Y0-DOK-378

# Reflections

A Guided Journal by GriefShare

This journal belongs to:

_____

Date:

_____

## Copyright

© MMXXI by Church Initiative. All rights reserved. Printed in the United States of America. Third printing, June MMXXV.

ISBN 979-8-9863655-3-4

No part of this book may be reproduced or transmitted in any form or by any means—including electronic, mechanical, photocopy, and recording—or by any information storage or retrieval system, without the written permission of the publisher.

All Scripture quotations, unless otherwise indicated, are taken from the Holy Bible, New International Version®, NIV®. Copyright ©1973, 1978, 1984, 2011 by Biblica, Inc.™ Used by permission of Zondervan. All rights reserved worldwide. www.zondervan.com The "NIV" and "New International Version" are trademarks registered in the United States Patent and Trademark Office by Biblica, Inc.™

Scripture quotations marked (NLT) are taken from the Holy Bible, New Living Translation, copyright © 1996, 2004, 2015 by Tyndale House Foundation. Used by permission of Tyndale House Publishers, a Division of Tyndale House Ministries, Carol Stream, Illinois 60188. All rights reserved.

The people quoted in this book have been featured in Church Initiative programs. If a last name is included, that person was interviewed as a grief recovery expert (counselor, pastor, author, etc.).

## Contact information:

Church Initiative
PO Box 1739
Wake Forest, NC 27588-1739

Phone: 800-395-5755 (US and Canada); 919-562-2112 (local and international)
Email: info@churchinitiative.org, info@griefshare.org
Web: churchinitiative.org, griefshare.org

# Contents

**Using Your Guided Journal**                     1
3 different sections for journaling

**Section 1: My Journey**                          11
Reflecting on your day-to-day life

**Section 2: Help Along the Way**                  93
Untangling your stresses one by one

    **The Shock of Grief**                         95
    **Fear & Anxiety**                            109
    **Relationships**                             123
    **Loneliness**                                137
    **Guilt & Anger**                             151
    **Stuck in Grief**                            165
    **Lessons Learned**                           179

**Section 3: Memories & Milestones**              193
Honoring the past & marking new growth

**Don't Grieve Alone**                            211
Experiencing God's presence

**How I Feel**                                    219
Words to help you describe emotions

**What Does the Bible Say?**                      223
Helpful verses for the grief journey

# Using your
## *Guided Journal*

### 3 different sections for journaling

This journal will help you take steps forward on your recovery journey. The sections guide you to reflect on your experiences in ways that can inspire hope and restore some balance in your life. Feel free to move around the book and journal on whatever page you'd like, whenever you'd like.

# Why this journal?

After the loss you've experienced, it's probably still difficult to process what has happened or what the future might look like. That's to be expected. Life can't be the same as it used to be.

Although it might be difficult to see this now, it is possible to get relief from the pain and even smile again. Think of your grief recovery as a **journey**. Like any journey, your recovery will take time, and you'll encounter twists and turns to navigate, hills to climb, and unmarked crossroads where decisions have to be made.

This guided journal will help you on this challenging, but necessary, journey. Unlike other journals, this one offers sections for different types of journaling, each of which can help you in different ways on your grief recovery journey. To get the most out of this book, take time to read the following descriptions and guidelines.

# *Using your journal*

**Each section is designed to help you take steps forward on your recovery journey and not get stuck or distracted along the way.**

## Section 1: My Journey
### Reflecting on your day-to-day life

*Questions*

Use these questions to guide you as you write about significant experiences or situations in your journal. See page 5 for more journaling tips.

1. What is—or has been—on your mind?

2. What challenges (or steps forward) did you experience today?

3. How did you feel about your challenges (or steps forward)? *(How I Feel guide, p. 219.)*

4. Did you make any significant decisions today? How did it go?

5. What does the Bible say about today's thoughts, feelings, and actions? *(What Does the Bible Say?, p. 223.)*

*Reflections*

In this section you'll write about what you went through on a particular day. The questions will guide you to reflect on your experiences in new ways that promote recovery.

Being able to process and reflect on your journey is critical to healing.

# Helpful *tips*

## Making the most of your experience

- **Don't simply describe events,** but also write what you were thinking, feeling, and wanting at the time.

- **Don't just blow off steam** as you journal. Honestly acknowledge what you've gone through, but then consider your difficulty from different angles (e.g., "What can I learn about myself through this?" or "How have family or friends helped me with this?").

- **Take a break if you feel overwhelmed** while writing; stop and come back to it later. Then start fresh by describing the facts of the situation, and ease into writing about your thoughts and feelings.

- **After traumatic experiences, wait** several days (or weeks) before writing about them to give yourself time to calm down.

- **Review past journal entries.** Look for patterns in your attitudes, emotions, and behaviors—both positive and negative.

- **Try rewriting earlier entries** from a different point of view (a more positive view, or a focus on what you've learned).

- **Record positive steps** in your healing: healthy choices you've made that will help you physically, emotionally, and spiritually.

# **Section 2:** Help Along the Way

## *Untangling your stresses one by one*

---

### HEARING FROM OTHERS

> "When my twin brother was
> killed, I heard it on the news,
> but I hoped it was somebody
> else. I was rather certain it was
> him, but I really hoped it wasn't.
> I didn't want to believe it."
>
> **LYNN**

> "I remember turning off all the
> lights and just dropping on the
> floor and asking God, 'Why?'"
>
> **GLENN**

### *Reflections*

In shock, Lynn found the news of her brother's death
hard to accept and Glenn cried out "Why?" How did
you initially respond to your loved one's death?

Accepting the fact that a loved one has died can be
extremely difficult. How have you tried to do this?

---

Stress can act like a thick fog that obscures your ability to see the path you need to be on. It can take the form of anger, anxiety, guilt, and loneliness.

This section contains journaling exercises to help you deal with your grief-related stresses. The personal stories and Bible passages will broaden your way of thinking as you reflect on your thoughts, feelings, and desires.

# Section 3: Memories & Milestones
## Honoring the past & marking new growth

Taking steps forward in your life does not mean forgetting your loved one. God brought you and your loved one together for His purposes. The blessings—and even the harder lessons from that relationship—should not be lost over time.

In section 3, you'll place mementos, pictures, and notes that will preserve your memory of the life you shared with one another.

On the Milestones pages you'll record accomplishments in your recovery journey, such as obstacles you've overcome or areas of personal growth.

# Need a little journaling *help?*

Use these sections (found in the back of the book) to help process your thoughts and feelings.

## Don't Grieve Alone

### Experiencing God's presence (p. 211)

Grief can be a lonely, painful process. You may wonder how God figures into your situation and where He is right now. Learn how God has made it possible for you to draw closer to Him—now and forever.

## How I Feel

### Words to help you describe your emotions (p. 219)

As you write, you may find you're struggling to translate your emotions into words. This word list will help you more accurately describe your feelings. Consider the different words and phrases that could be used for different emotions. Pick those that seem to best match your experience.

## What Does the Bible Say?

### Helpful verses for the grief journey (p. 223)

The Bible verses found in this section are available to help you view and process your struggles in new, helpful ways. God offers a perspective that exceeds our limited ability to make sense of trials. God truly cares for you, and He understands and empathizes with your pain.

# More *help* along the way

Your guided journal is just one of many tools available to help you grow and heal on your journey. If you'd like additional support and encouragement, here are four more helpful resources available for you:

- **GriefShare group** – This support group provides counsel and helpful tips from experts and people who've been through grief. Groups meet in person and online. **griefshare.org**

- **GriefShare.org** – You can find various resources to help with your questions and grief-related struggles.

- **Surviving the Holidays** – Around Thanksgiving and Christmas, this video-based seminar will help you face the holidays after a loss. griefshare.org/holidays

- **Loss of a Spouse** – This 2-hour seminar (offered online and in person) is designed for people who are grieving the loss of their spouse. griefshare.org/loss

# My Journey

## Reflecting on your day-to-day life

Your grief can take you down unexpected roads; it can be easy to feel lost or like you're walking in circles. Use the questions in this section as a way to find clarity and direction for situations you face each day or to reflect on how you're doing overall. You could write about a frustrating moment, a worry, a conflict, or questions you're wrestling with. Or, write about something positive that happened or a healthy choice you made.

# Questions

Use these questions to help you write about your experiences today, or overall. For each entry in this section, pick one or two (or more) to write about. See tips on page 5.

1. What is—or has been—on your mind?

2. What challenges (or steps forward) did you experience today?

3. How did you feel about your challenges (or steps forward)? *(How I Feel, p. 219.)*

4. Did you make any significant decisions today? How did it go?

5. What does the Bible say about your thoughts, feelings, and actions? *(What Does the Bible Say?, p. 223.)*

# Reflections

## QUESTIONS

1. What's on your mind?
2. Challenges (or steps forward)?
3. How did you feel?
   **(Feelings guide, p. 219)**
4. Significant decisions?
5. What does the Bible say?
   **(Topical guide, p. 223)**

TIP | You don't need to go through this journal "in order." Write on whatever page you'd like, whenever you'd like.

# Reflections

_____ / _____ / _____

# QUESTIONS

1. What's on your mind?
2. Challenges (or steps forward)?
3. How did you feel?
   **(Feelings guide, p. 219)**
4. Significant decisions?
5. What does the Bible say?
   **(Topical guide, p. 223)**

# Reflections

_____ / _____ / _____

# QUESTIONS

1. What's on your mind?
2. Challenges (or steps forward)?
3. How did you feel?
   **(Feelings guide, p. 219)**
4. Significant decisions?
5. What does the Bible say?
   **(Topical guide, p. 223)**

**TIP** | Don't worry about spelling or grammar as you write.

# Reflections

_____ / _____ / _____

# QUESTIONS

1. What's on your mind?
2. Challenges (or steps forward)?
3. How did you feel?
   **(Feelings guide, p. 219)**
4. Significant decisions?
5. What does the Bible say?
   **(Topical guide, p. 223)**

# Reflections

_____ / _____ / _____

# QUESTIONS

1. What's on your mind?
2. Challenges (or steps forward)?
3. How did you feel?
   **(Feelings guide, p. 219)**
4. Significant decisions?
5. What does the Bible say?
   **(Topical guide, p. 223)**

# Reflections

_____ / _____ / _____

## QUESTIONS

1. What's on your mind?
2. Challenges (or steps forward)?
3. How did you feel?
   **(Feelings guide, p. 219)**
4. Significant decisions?
5. What does the Bible say?
   **(Topical guide, p. 223)**

**TIP** There's no "prescribed" number of times you need to journal. Do what suits you and your schedule.

# Reflections

# QUESTIONS

1. What's on your mind?
2. Challenges (or steps forward)?
3. How did you feel?
   **(Feelings guide, p. 219)**
4. Significant decisions?
5. What does the Bible say?
   **(Topical guide, p. 223)**

# Reflections

# QUESTIONS

1. What's on your mind?
2. Challenges (or steps forward)?
3. How did you feel?
   **(Feelings guide, p. 219)**
4. Significant decisions?
5. What does the Bible say?
   **(Topical guide, p. 223)**

# Reflections

_____ / _____ / _____

# QUESTIONS

1. What's on your mind?
2. Challenges (or steps forward)?
3. How did you feel?
   **(Feelings guide, p. 219)**
4. Significant decisions?
5. What does the Bible say?
   **(Topical guide, p. 223)**

# Reflections

# QUESTIONS

1. What's on your mind?
2. Challenges (or steps forward)?
3. How did you feel?
   **(Feelings guide, p. 219)**
4. Significant decisions?
5. What does the Bible say?
   **(Topical guide, p. 223)**

# Reflections

# QUESTIONS

1. What's on your mind?
2. Challenges (or steps forward)?
3. How did you feel?
   **(Feelings guide, p. 219)**
4. Significant decisions?
5. What does the Bible say?
   **(Topical guide, p. 223)**

# Reflections

_____ / _____ / _____

# QUESTIONS

1. What's on your mind?
2. Challenges (or steps forward)?
3. How did you feel?
   **(Feelings guide, p. 219)**
4. Significant decisions?
5. What does the Bible say?
   **(Topical guide, p. 223)**

# Reflections

## QUESTIONS

1. What's on your mind?
2. Challenges (or steps forward)?
3. How did you feel?
   **(Feelings guide, p. 219)**
4. Significant decisions?
5. What does the Bible say?
   **(Topical guide, p. 223)**

**TIP** It's okay to start writing on one topic and find that your train of thought takes you to another topic.

# Reflections

# QUESTIONS

1. What's on your mind?
2. Challenges (or steps forward)?
3. How did you feel?
   **(Feelings guide, p. 219)**
4. Significant decisions?
5. What does the Bible say?
   **(Topical guide, p. 223)**

# Reflections

# QUESTIONS

1. What's on your mind?
2. Challenges (or steps forward)?
3. How did you feel?
   **(Feelings guide, p. 219)**
4. Significant decisions?
5. What does the Bible say?
   **(Topical guide, p. 223)**

# Reflections

# QUESTIONS

1. What's on your mind?
2. Challenges (or steps forward)?
3. How did you feel?
   **(Feelings guide, p. 219)**
4. Significant decisions?
5. What does the Bible say?
   **(Topical guide, p. 223)**

# Reflections

# QUESTIONS

1. What's on your mind?
2. Challenges (or steps forward)?
3. How did you feel?
   **(Feelings guide, p. 219)**
4. Significant decisions?
5. What does the Bible say?
   **(Topical guide, p. 223)**

# Reflections

# QUESTIONS

1. What's on your mind?
2. Challenges (or steps forward)?
3. How did you feel?
   **(Feelings guide, p. 219)**
4. Significant decisions?
5. What does the Bible say?
   **(Topical guide, p. 223)**

# Reflections

# QUESTIONS

1. What's on your mind?
2. Challenges (or steps forward)?
3. How did you feel?
   **(Feelings guide, p. 219)**
4. Significant decisions?
5. What does the Bible say?
   **(Topical guide, p. 223)**

**TIP** | Pray for God to use your journal to help you heal.

# Reflections

# QUESTIONS

1. What's on your mind?
2. Challenges (or steps forward)?
3. How did you feel?
   **(Feelings guide, p. 219)**
4. Significant decisions?
5. What does the Bible say?
   **(Topical guide, p. 223)**

# Reflections

_____ / _____ / _____

# QUESTIONS

1. What's on your mind?
2. Challenges (or steps forward)?
3. How did you feel?
   **(Feelings guide, p. 219)**
4. Significant decisions?
5. What does the Bible say?
   **(Topical guide, p. 223)**

Reflections

_____ / _____ / _____

# QUESTIONS

1. What's on your mind?
2. Challenges (or steps forward)?
3. How did you feel?
   **(Feelings guide, p. 219)**
4. Significant decisions?
5. What does the Bible say?
   **(Topical guide, p. 223)**

# Reflections

_____ / _____ / _____

# QUESTIONS

1. What's on your mind?
2. Challenges (or steps forward)?
3. How did you feel?
   **(Feelings guide, p. 219)**
4. Significant decisions?
5. What does the Bible say?
   **(Topical guide, p. 223)**

# Reflections

_____ / _____ / _____

# QUESTIONS

1. What's on your mind?
2. Challenges (or steps forward)?
3. How did you feel?
   **(Feelings guide, p. 219)**
4. Significant decisions?
5. What does the Bible say?
   **(Topical guide, p. 223)**

_____ / _____ / _____

# QUESTIONS

1. What's on your mind?
2. Challenges (or steps forward)?
3. How did you feel?
   **(Feelings guide, p. 219)**
4. Significant decisions?
5. What does the Bible say?
   **(Topical guide, p. 223)**

# Reflections

___ / ___ / ___

## QUESTIONS

1. What's on your mind?
2. Challenges (or steps forward)?
3. How did you feel?
   **(Feelings guide, p. 219)**
4. Significant decisions?
5. What does the Bible say?
   **(Topical guide, p. 223)**

**TIP** | Read a previous entry and write about what you've realized or learned since writing it.

# Reflections

_____ / _____ / _____

# QUESTIONS

1. What's on your mind?
2. Challenges (or steps forward)?
3. How did you feel?
   **(Feelings guide, p. 219)**
4. Significant decisions?
5. What does the Bible say?
   **(Topical guide, p. 223)**

# Reflections

# QUESTIONS

1. What's on your mind?
2. Challenges (or steps forward)?
3. How did you feel?
   **(Feelings guide, p. 219)**
4. Significant decisions?
5. What does the Bible say?
   **(Topical guide, p. 223)**

# Reflections

____ / ____ / ____

# QUESTIONS

1. What's on your mind?
2. Challenges (or steps forward)?
3. How did you feel?
   **(Feelings guide, p. 219)**
4. Significant decisions?
5. What does the Bible say?
   **(Topical guide, p. 223)**

# Reflections

# QUESTIONS

1. What's on your mind?
2. Challenges (or steps forward)?
3. How did you feel?
   **(Feelings guide, p. 219)**
4. Significant decisions?
5. What does the Bible say?
   **(Topical guide, p. 223)**

# Reflections

_____ / _____ / _____

## QUESTIONS

1. What's on your mind?
2. Challenges (or steps forward)?
3. How did you feel?
   **(Feelings guide, p. 219)**
4. Significant decisions?
5. What does the Bible say?
   **(Topical guide, p. 223)**

# Reflections

## QUESTIONS

1. What's on your mind?
2. Challenges (or steps forward)?
3. How did you feel?
   **(Feelings guide, p. 219)**
4. Significant decisions?
5. What does the Bible say?
   **(Topical guide, p. 223)**

# Reflections

# QUESTIONS

1. What's on your mind?
2. Challenges (or steps forward)?
3. How did you feel?
   **(Feelings guide, p. 219)**
4. Significant decisions?
5. What does the Bible say?
   **(Topical guide, p. 223)**

**TIP** | Try writing your journal entry as a prayer to God. Tell Him what's going on and ask for His help.

# Reflections

## QUESTIONS

1. What's on your mind?
2. Challenges (or steps forward)?
3. How did you feel?
   **(Feelings guide, p. 219)**
4. Significant decisions?
5. What does the Bible say?
   **(Topical guide, p. 223)**

# Reflections

# QUESTIONS

1. What's on your mind?
2. Challenges (or steps forward)?
3. How did you feel?
   **(Feelings guide, p. 219)**
4. Significant decisions?
5. What does the Bible say?
   **(Topical guide, p. 223)**

# Reflections

# QUESTIONS

1. What's on your mind?
2. Challenges (or steps forward)?
3. How did you feel?
   **(Feelings guide, p. 219)**
4. Significant decisions?
5. What does the Bible say?
   **(Topical guide, p. 223)**

# Reflections

_____ / _____ / _____

## QUESTIONS

1. What's on your mind?
2. Challenges (or steps forward)?
3. How did you feel?
   **(Feelings guide, p. 219)**
4. Significant decisions?
5. What does the Bible say?
   **(Topical guide, p. 223)**

# Reflections

_____ / _____ / _____

# QUESTIONS

1. What's on your mind?
2. Challenges (or steps forward)?
3. How did you feel?
   **(Feelings guide, p. 219)**
4. Significant decisions?
5. What does the Bible say?
   **(Topical guide, p. 223)**

# Reflections

_____ / _____ / _____

## QUESTIONS

1. What's on your mind?
2. Challenges (or steps forward)?
3. How did you feel?
   **(Feelings guide, p. 219)**
4. Significant decisions?
5. What does the Bible say?
   **(Topical guide, p. 223)**

**TIP** Go back and read previous entries to see how much you've grown.

# Reflections

_____ / _____ / _____

# Help Along the Way

## Untangling your stresses one by one

Walking unfamiliar roads is challenging, but having a road map can help! In this journaling section, you'll hear from other people who have traveled before you. They share lessons they've learned throughout their grief process that you, too, might apply. You'll also discover Bible passages that will help you avoid unnecessary detours and make wise decisions along the way.

# The Shock of *Grief*

Hearing the news sends shock waves through every area of your life. It hits everyone differently, but it's common to feel the shock physically, emotionally, mentally, and spiritually. This period of numbness and confusion can last for several days after the loss. Consider how grief has affected your whole person.

"Everything I did was kind of robotic. …
Everything was going in slow motion."

JEMMA

# Hearing from others

"When my twin brother was killed, I heard it on the news, but I hoped it was somebody else. I was rather certain it was him, but I really hoped it wasn't. I didn't want to believe it."

**LYNN**

"I remember turning off all the lights and just dropping on the floor and asking God, 'Why?'"

**GLENN**

# Reflections

**In shock, Lynn found the news of her brother's death hard to accept and Glenn cried out "Why?" How did you initially respond to your loved one's death?**

_____

_____

_____

_____

_____

**What evidence is there that you have begun to accept— or are in denial about—your loved one's death?**

_____

_____

_____

_____

_____

# Hearing from God

Listen to my words, LORD,
consider my lament. Hear my
cry for help, my King and my God,
for to you I pray.

**PSALM 5:1–2**

Do not be far from me,
my God; come quickly,
God, to help me.

**PSALM 71:12**

# Reflections

**The psalmists cried out to God for help. Use this space to tell God about how the shock of loss has affected you, and to ask for His help.**

God, _____

_____

_____

_____

_____

_____

_____

_____

_____

_____

# My Journey

Write about the shock of grief or
anything else on your heart.

**Cast all your anxiety on him because he cares for you.**

1 PETER 5:7

# Hearing from others

"It seemed like God pushed the pause button on my life and it's just like everything stopped."

**SHARON**

"I knew what two police officers at my door meant, and I really had no feeling at all. Just numbness."

**MOLLY**

# Reflections

**How do you relate to Sharon's and Molly's experiences with the shock of loss? What has your experience been like?**

_____

_____

_____

_____

**What have you found helpful as you've faced the initial days and weeks after your loved one's death? Or what do you think might be helpful?**

_____

_____

_____

_____

# Hearing from God

The LORD is close to the

## *brokenhearted*

and saves those who

are crushed in spirit.

**PSALM 34:18**

# Reflections

**How are you feeling deep down? What has grief done to your heart and spirit?**

---

---

---

---

---

**What do you think about the statement that God is "close to the brokenhearted"?**

---

---

---

---

---

# My Journey

Write about the shock of grief or
anything else on your heart.

_____

_____

_____

_____

_____

_____

_____

_____

_____

_____

_____

_____

_____

**Turn to me and be gracious to me, for I am lonely and afflicted.**

# Fear & *Anxiety*

Your life is forever changed. Perhaps you're dealing with new fears and worries every day. Try using this section to reflect on what is making you fearful or anxious and to find ways to help you cope with those struggles.

**"I kept a journal and would record how much anxiety I had that day."**

**ROB**

# Hearing from others

"I was fearful of what was going to happen to my kids and me."

**MARISOL**

"I had anxiety about being alone."

**CAROLYN**

"I'm always scared now that something's going to happen to somebody else."

**JODY**

# Reflections

_____ / _____ / _____

## What kind of fears has your loss generated? How have you dealt with them?

### Where to *turn*

Find help at GriefShare. Join a group today.
**griefshare.org**

# Hearing from God

The LORD is my rock, my fortress, and my savior; my God is my rock, in whom I find protection. He is my shield, the power that saves me, and my place of safety.

**PSALM 18:2 (NLT)**

God is our refuge and strength, always ready to help in times of trouble.

**PSALM 46:1 (NLT)**

# Reflections

**When challenges come, who or what do you turn to when you are anxious or afraid? Share how this has helped or hurt you.**

# My Journey

Write about your fears and anxieties or anything else you'd like to express.

Fear of man will prove to be a snare,
but whoever trusts in the LORD is kept safe.

**PROVERBS 29:25**

# Hearing from others

"I started thinking about things that I could possibly face in the future, when I wouldn't have Kath with me to help."

**ROB**

# Reflections

## How has your loved one's death meant a loss of support in your life?

## How are you seeking needed support now?

# Hearing from God

Even when I walk

through the darkest valley,

I will not be afraid, for

## *you are close*

beside me. Your rod and your staff

protect and comfort me.

**PSALM 23:4 (NLT)**

*Reflections*

**God is near to those who cry out to Him, even when they don't "feel" His presence in the dark valley. How have you experienced God's presence?**

**Do you feel protected and comforted? Why or why not?**

# My Journey

Write about your fears and anxieties or
anything else you'd like to express.

So do not fear, for I am with you; do not be dismayed,
for I am your God. I will strengthen you and help you;
I will uphold you with my righteous right hand.

# Relationships

Grief can put a strain on relationships. Some of your friends and relatives will be struggling with their own grief, which can distract them from their relationship with you. Others simply might not know how to talk with you. Here are some journaling prompts to help you work through the challenges in relationships that you might face during your journey.

# Hearing from others

"Sometimes people say things in a way that implies I should be okay and not grieve anymore, like, 'Hey, he's in heaven. Move on.' It's hard to know how to respond to that. I want to say 'That didn't help me at all!' I guess they're trying to bring an eternal perspective, but they need to understand that our sadness isn't about eternity, it's about our present life without our loved one in it."

**CARLA**

# Reflections

**Think about some of the unhelpful responses you've received and how you reacted. What might be a more gracious way for you to respond in the future?**

---

---

---

---

---

---

---

---

---

## In a GriefShare *group?*

You don't have to go through this alone.
Find a group today (in person or online).
**griefshare.org**

# Hearing from God

Like one who takes

away a garment on a cold day, or

like vinegar poured on a wound,

is one who sings songs to a

*heavy heart.*

PROVERBS 25:20

# Reflections

**Unfortunately, not everyone will be patient with your grief journey. How have you felt pressured to act a certain way?**

_____

_____

_____

_____

_____

**What has been your response to these challenges in your relationships?**

_____

_____

_____

_____

_____

# My Journey

Write about how grief has affected your relationships or anything else that's on your mind.

Bear with each other and forgive one another if any of you has a
grievance against someone. Forgive as the Lord forgave you.

**COLOSSIANS 3:13**

# Hearing from God

Each heart knows its

own bitterness, and no

one else can share its joy.

**PROVERBS 14:10**

# Reflections

**In what ways have other people's responses to your loss seemed hard to understand?**

**In light of this verse, reflect on why people make insensitive (although usually well-meaning) comments.**

# Hearing from others

"Be whoever you are.
Your own pattern of grief will
be your pattern of grief."

**DR. LARRY CRABB**

"Recognize that all the family
members are grieving at their
own pace and in their own way."

**SUSAN K. BEENEY, RN**

# Reflections

**What's it like for you to grieve around other people?**

_____

_____

_____

_____

_____

**How are other people around you handling your grief (and theirs)?**

_____

_____

_____

_____

_____

# My Journey

Write about how grief has affected your relationships or anything else that's on your mind.

**A hot-tempered person stirs up conflict,
but the one who is patient calms a quarrel.**
PROVERBS 15:18

# Loneliness

The loneliness that occurs after the death of a loved one is painful to bear and hard for other people to understand. Maybe you've tried to fill the emptiness, but without success. When you feel lonely, turn to these pages to let out those feelings and to find encouragement and hope.

**"She isn't there to talk to, and I feel all alone."**

DAVID

## Turn to me

and be gracious to me,

for I am lonely and afflicted.

Relieve the troubles of my heart

and free me from my anguish.

**PSALM 25:16–17**

# Reflections

**When you are alone, what troubles weigh heavily on you?**

_____

_____

_____

_____

_____

**How would you like God to help you with them?**

_____

_____

_____

_____

_____

# Hearing from others

"I can still remember that first night going to bed alone, and as I closed the door in my room, I remember just crying out two words to God, 'Help me.' And you know, He did."

**JOYCE**

# Reflections

**Do you cry out to God when you feel lonely? Why or why not?**

**In what ways has God helped you so far on your recovery journey?**

# My Journey

Express your thoughts on loneliness or any other challenges you're facing.

Even though I walk through the darkest valley, I will fear no evil, for you are with me; your rod and your staff, they comfort me.

**PSALM 23:4**

# Hearing from others

"There will be some lonely nights and some lonely moments, but realize that God is always there. When we think about Him as Immanuel, which means God with us, we realize that He really is an ever-present help in times of trouble."

**SABRINA BLACK**

# Reflections

**What are some things you do when you feel lonely? How helpful have you found those responses?**

**When you think about the truth that God is always with you, how does that affect your perspective on loneliness?**

# Hearing from God

*The Lord himself*

goes before you and will be with

you; he will never leave you nor

forsake you. Do not be afraid.

**DEUTERONOMY 31:8A**

# Reflections

**How often do you think about God when you are feeling lonely? What thoughts do you have?**

**What might help you connect to God at these times?**

You're not *alone*

Join a GriefShare group today to get connected and encouraged (groups are in person or online).
**griefshare.org**

# My Journey

Express your thoughts on loneliness or any
other challenges you're facing.

**A father to the fatherless, a defender of widows,
is God in his holy dwelling.**

# Guilt & *Anger*

Regret. Rage. Remorse. These emotions can consume us. They eat us up from the inside out, preventing healing as they steal away peace and comfort. When you're struggling with these feelings, use this section to work through these powerful emotions in beneficial ways.

# Hearing from God

My guilt has overwhelmed me like a
burden too heavy to bear. ... LORD,

## *do not forsake me;*

do not be far from me, my God.

Come quickly to help me,

my Lord and my Savior.

**PSALM 38:4, 21–22**

# Reflections

**Pour out on this page anything you're feeling guilty about. What impact has holding on to this guilt had in your life?**

# Hearing from God

You, Lord, are forgiving and good, abounding in love to all who call to you. Hear my prayer, LORD; listen to my cry for mercy.

**PSALM 86:5–6**

If you, LORD, kept a record of sins, Lord, who could stand? But with you there is forgiveness, so that we can, with reverence, serve you.

**PSALM 130:3–4**

# Reflections

**Describe your reaction to God's assurance of forgiveness. Write your thoughts as a prayer to God.**

# My Journey

Express your thoughts on guilt and anger in your life.
Or write about other challenges you're going through.

If we confess our sins, he is faithful and just and will forgive
us our sins and purify us from all unrighteousness.
**1 JOHN 1:9**

# Hearing from others

"After I came to the Lord, I realized, 'If He could forgive, then surely I could forgive.' It took a long time, but I realized I needed to do that. I also realized that Kyle didn't die because of my sins, and I started to feel a lot of that guilt being relieved. Forgiving has relieved a very heavy load off my shoulders. Every human is not perfect. I'm not perfect. I realized that could have been me driving that truck. Forgiveness is definitely a process."

**JOANNE**

# Reflections

**How has unforgiveness affected your life?**

_____

_____

_____

_____

_____

**How have you dealt with upsetting issues that have come up since your loved one's death?**

_____

_____

_____

_____

# Hearing from others

"One minute, I was praising the Lord that I had a child safe in His kingdom and thanking Him for providing a way for us. The next moment, I was angry with God for taking my baby."

**SHARON**

# Reflections

**Is your sorrow mixed with anger? What are you angry about, and how is it affecting you?**

### Find *peace*

If you'd like more help dealing with guilt and anger,
join a GriefShare group today.
**griefshare.org**

GUILT & ANGER

161

# My Journey

Express your thoughts on guilt and anger in your life.
Or write about other challenges you're going through.

Therefore, there is now no condemnation for those who are in Christ Jesus.

**ROMANS 8:1**

# Stuck in *Grief*

Sometimes people feel "stuck" in grief and unable to move forward. Problems can arise if you try to numb the pain with unhealthy choices, refuse to make changes after a death, get embittered, or can't shake the feeling of being totally lost or abandoned. Journaling can help you think about your loss and its impact rather than denying, ignoring, or numbing the pain.

# Hearing from others

"Grief can freeze you in place. [Refusing to deal with your emotions] can trap you in a prison of your own making. In the North, when the frost of the season comes, the lakes begin to ice over. At this point, the ice can still be broken or thawed.
But as the winter progresses, layers of ice build up until the lake is so solid that even a truck can drive across it. Like the lake, over time, you can become frozen in layer after layer of grief if you do not deal with your emotions as they come."

**DR. JOHN TRENT**

# Reflections

## Describe any ways you feel frozen in grief.

---

---

---

---

---

---

---

---

---

---

### In a GriefShare *group?*

You don't have to go through this alone.
Find a group today (in person or online).

**griefshare.org**

## Be merciful

to me, LORD, for I am in distress;

my eyes grow weak with sorrow,

my soul and body with grief.

**PSALM 31:9**

# Reflections

**In what ways would you like God to show you His mercy?**

# My Journey

Write your thoughts on being stuck in grief or anything else you've been dealing with.

Why, my soul, are you downcast? Why so disturbed within me?
Put your hope in God, for I will yet praise him, my Savior and my God.

PSALM 42:5

# Hearing from others

"Grief is like a heavy weight on me some days, where I can't even get dressed. I can't even get out of bed. It's hard for me to see what's down the road. I have no clue. But all I know is, I'm ready for something more. I want something more. And I feel like God has something for me."

**SHAY**

# Reflections

**In what ways can you relate to Shay?**

**What signs are there that God has something for you on the road ahead?**

# Hearing from God

For I am convinced that neither death nor life, neither angels nor demons, neither the present nor the future, nor any powers, neither height nor depth, nor anything else in all creation, will be able to separate us from the love of God that is in Christ Jesus our Lord.

**ROMANS 8:38–39**

"He will wipe every tear from their eyes. There will be no more death" or mourning or crying or pain, for the old order of things has passed away.

**REVELATION 21:4**

# Reflections

**What hope do these verses offer when you feel like your grief will never end?**

# My Journey

Write your thoughts on being stuck in grief or anything else you've been dealing with.

We wait in hope for the LORD; he is our help and our shield. In him our hearts rejoice, for we trust in his holy name. May your unfailing love be with us, LORD, even as we put our hope in you.

**PSALM 33:20–22**

# Lessons *Learned*

Grief can be revealing. It can teach us many things—about ourselves, about others, and about life. What have you discovered about yourself on this journey? About your family and friends? Use this section to reflect on the lessons you've learned.

**"God never wastes our sorrows."**

DR. JOSEPH STOWELL

# Hearing from God

And the God of all grace,
who called you to his

## *eternal glory*

in Christ, after you have
suffered a little while, will himself
restore you and make you strong,
firm and steadfast.

**1 PETER 5:10**

# Reflections

**Have you noticed any ways that your grief has made you stronger?**

<br>

_____

_____

_____

_____

_____

_____

_____

_____

_____

_____

## Go deeper

Receive support and guidance for your grief journey.

**griefshare.org**

# Hearing from others

"When you're so full of sorrow, not knowing which way to turn, it shows you that everything else doesn't make any difference. What really matters is eternity."

**LORRAINE**

# Reflections

**How have your thoughts about eternity (or other matters of "ultimate concern") been affected by your grief journey?**

_____

_____

_____

_____

_____

**How can the things you've learned help you in the future?**

_____

_____

_____

_____

_____

# My Journey

Reflect on lessons you've learned throughout this grief process. Or write about anything else on your heart.

**Come to me, all you who are weary and burdened, and I will give you rest.**

# Hearing from God

Praise be to the God and Father of our Lord Jesus Christ, the Father of compassion and the

## God of all comfort,

who comforts us in all our troubles, so that we can comfort those in any trouble with the comfort we ourselves receive from God.

**2 CORINTHIANS 1:3–4**

# Reflections

**Describe any comfort from the Lord that you've experienced while grieving.**

**How can the things you've learned help you in the future?**

# Hearing from others

"Sometimes the best remedy for grief is finding some way to touch somebody else's life."

**DR. LARRY CRABB**

*Reflections*

**Describe any opportunities you've had to touch others' lives (helped or encouraged them), even in the midst of your grief.**

# My Journey

Reflect on lessons you've learned throughout this grief process. Or write about anything else on your heart.

But the Lord is faithful, and he will strengthen you
and protect you from the evil one.

**2 THESSALONIANS 3:3**

# Memories & Milestones

## Honoring the past & marking new growth

*Memorabilia* are the things that help you remember your loved one, such as cards, letters, or pictures. *Milestones* are significant markers of progress on your journey without your loved one. In this section of your journal, you'll collect and reflect on special memories. You'll also record significant steps forward that you've taken as you move ahead with your life.

# Memories

The following pages are free space to bring together and preserve memories of your loved one. Attach pictures, memorabilia, or notes. Write about significant experiences you had together.

Tip: Use tape rather than glue to protect your journal pages and memorabilia.

**"A memory is a photograph taken by the heart to make a special moment last forever."**

UNKNOWN

# Notes

# Notes

_____
_____
_____
_____
_____
_____
_____
_____
_____
_____
_____
_____
_____
_____
_____
_____
_____

# Notes

_____
_____
_____
_____
_____
_____
_____
_____
_____
_____
_____
_____
_____
_____
_____
_____
_____

# Notes

# Milestones

A milestone sits at the side of the road, to tell you where you are, how far you've come, and what might be coming next. What milestones are you seeing in your life? You might record the first time you were able to return to a favorite restaurant the two of you frequented or a time when you accomplished a task you would have not thought possible in the past. You could write about a new hobby you've started to pursue or a positive decision you've made. Such milestones mark where obstacles were overcome and where areas of personal growth reinvigorated life after loss.

# Tracking My *Journey*

1. _____ ___/___/___

   _____

2. _____ ___/___/___

   _____

3. _____ ___/___/___

   _____

4. _____ ___/___/___

   _____

5. _____ ___/___/___

   _____

6. _____ ___/___/___

   _____

7. _____ ___/___/___

   _____

8. _____ ___/___/___

   _____

9. _____ ___/___/___

   _____

10. _____ ___/___/___

_____

11. _____ ___/___/___

_____

12. _____ ___/___/___

_____

13. _____ ___/___/___

_____

14. _____ ___/___/___

_____

15. _____ ___/___/___

_____

16. _____ ___/___/___

_____

17. _____ ___/___/___

_____

18. _____ ___/___/___

_____

19. _____ ___/___/___

_____

**20.** _____ __/__/__

**21.** _____ __/__/__

**22.** _____ __/__/__

**23.** _____ __/__/__

**24.** _____ __/__/__

**25.** _____ __/__/__

**26.** _____ __/__/__

**27.** _____ __/__/__

**28.** _____ __/__/__

**29.** _____ __/__/__

30. _____ ___ / ___ / ___

_____

31. _____ ___ / ___ / ___

_____

32. _____ ___ / ___ / ___

_____

33. _____ ___ / ___ / ___

_____

34. _____ ___ / ___ / ___

_____

35. _____ ___ / ___ / ___

_____

36. _____ ___ / ___ / ___

_____

37. _____ ___ / ___ / ___

_____

38. _____ ___ / ___ / ___

_____

39. _____ ___ / ___ / ___

_____

# Don't Grieve Alone

## Experiencing God's presence

In your grief, you might be wondering, "Where is God now? How do I receive His comfort?" This section talks about how you can know God and draw closer to Him in your grief.

**Let us then approach God's throne of grace with confidence, so that we may receive mercy and find grace to help us in our time of need.**

**HEBREWS 4:16**

# Who do you turn to in grief?

As you've reflected on the impact of your loved one's death, you've had an opportunity to wrestle with some incredibly painful emotions and thoughts. Perhaps you've felt like Christina, who lost her sister to cancer.

*"My sister's death was the most painful experience I'd ever had in my life. I felt I could not go on and that I needed her with me. Why her? Why did we have to have this loss?"*
– CHRISTINA

All the changes and the uncertainties you're left with could easily lead you to a sense of desperation. Where can you turn with such desperation? Perhaps friends? Supportive friends and relatives can be a wonderful blessing, but they will always be limited in what they can do to help.

*"After my son died, people were saying, 'Oh, I'm so sorry,' but they didn't understand the hurt, and I guess I wanted more from them. I just wanted them to feel what I felt, and of course, there was no way for them to do that."*
– PHOEBE

# Where is God in all of this?

What about God? He's supposed to be able to help like no one else can, but will He? After Stephen's wife died, he struggled to figure out how God fit into his desperate situation.

*"My faith and trust in the Lord just went out the window after my wife's death, and I would have nothing to do with God. I could have cared less about anything else except my daughter and grandchildren. ... One night I was leaning up against the wall, and I looked around in this big old house, and I remember saying, 'Lord, I'm in this darn house all by myself!' And I let it rip. I mean, for 20 or 30 minutes, blue smoke was coming out of my mouth. 'Where are You? You don't care! You don't understand!'"* – **STEPHEN**

According to the Bible, it is true that God can help us in our distress. "Ah, Sovereign LORD, you have made the heavens and the earth by your great power and outstretched arm. Nothing is too hard for you" (Jeremiah 32:17).

# God is near

God's help comes through a relationship with Him. "For the eyes of the LORD range throughout the earth to strengthen those whose hearts are fully committed to him" (2 Chronicles 16:9a).

*"God has a master plan: We have a part in it, and He's with us through it all. Slowly but surely I was able to let go of my anger and receive His love and strength. Just because I didn't see my sister's death coming does not mean God was taken by surprise. He knew we would be at this place, and He was with me during the grieving process. So, I couldn't continue to be angry at Him, because I knew He was with me."* – **CHRISTINA**

*"One day I went to a store just to get my mind off my grief. [A song came on] that was played at Matthew's funeral. I stopped where I was and just broke down. I did not care who was looking at me. I poured out my heart to God. I bawled my eyes out. God's comfort surrounded me, and I knew I wasn't alone. God was with me in my grief. He knew what I was going through because God lost His Son, Jesus."*

– PHOEBE

## What's getting in the way?

Obviously, not everyone has the kind of relationship with God that Christina and Phoebe have (and countless others throughout history). How did they develop this kind of relationship with God?

It starts with recognizing a simple truth: We're all prone to ignore (and rebel against!) God. It's true of us all because, in biblical terms, we are all "sinners." That's why when life is difficult, we often blame or rail against God. And when life goes the way we want, we often forget about God or disregard what He has to say in the Bible. The Bible calls our rebellion against and our apathy toward God *sin*.

Sadly, sin creates a barrier between God and us that we can't penetrate. While this prevents us from knowing God and receiving His help, He made a way to break down this barrier so that we can be in relationship with Him.

## How things are made right

According to God's great love, He sent His own Son, Jesus, to earth to remove the barrier between us and God. Jesus lived a perfect life and experienced a terrible death, so that through His resurrection we could receive forgiveness and eternal life with Him. Through our belief in Jesus, God makes it possible for us to have a real relationship with Him—the kind that has blessed and comforted people like Christina, Phoebe, and many others.

## Comfort for your grief

Because of Jesus, you can start this kind of comforting relationship with the Lord. All you have to do is:

- Acknowledge you are a sinner (someone who ignores and has disobeyed God)
- Acknowledge that Jesus is your Savior from sin
- Ask God for forgiveness of your sins
- Commit to following God's will and direction for your life (as revealed in the Bible)

**Take some time now to write out your prayer to God, including the above four points in your prayer:**

___ / ___ / ___

# Next steps for your journey

Talk with a pastor, a mature Christian friend, or someone on your GriefShare ministry team about your new relationship with Jesus. He or she can help you figure out the next steps you need to take to deepen this relationship.

Eventually Stephen realized that turning away from the Lord was actually hindering him as he dealt with the death of his wife. Here's more of his story:

*"Since Sandy's death, I've grown to trust God. There's nothing that is totally in our control. We can think it's in our control, but we just have to turn it over to the Lord. He wants us to have a relationship with Him every day and to trust that He's guiding our footsteps. He didn't guarantee us a painless road for life, but He did guarantee to help us with every step on it. He's there. And all we have to do is continually trust Him, believe in Him, and ask for His guidance."* – **STEPHEN**

# How I Feel

## Words to help you describe emotions

If an experience you've had is hard to get out of your mind, and difficult to put into words, here are words you could use for different types of emotions.

## Anger

Enraged
Furious
Resentful
Ticked off
Fed up
Irritated
Aggravated
Offended
Impatient
Annoyed

## Fear

Horrified
Petrified
Panicky
Frantic
Unsafe
Intimidated
On edge
Skittish
Apprehensive
Nervous

## Sadness

Hopeless
In despair
Miserable
Devastated
Crushed
Distraught
Weepy
Sorrowful
Gloomy
Heartbroken
Downcast

## Joy

Jubilant
Overjoyed
Ecstatic
Exhilarated
Thrilled
In high spirits
Enthusiastic
Giddy
Glad
Grateful
Delighted
Pleased

## Shame/Guilt

Humiliated
Remorseful
Ashamed
Regretful
Contrite
Sorry
Sheepish
Embarrassed

## Surprise

Awestruck
Amazed
Astonished
Shocked
Stunned
Startled
Alarmed

## Comfort

Blessed
Hopeful
Contented
Peaceful
Secure
Tranquil
Calm
At ease
Relaxed
Loved
Nurtured
Cared for

# What Does
## *the Bible Say?*

Turn to these pages to find helpful Bible verses that are related to the struggles you may be facing. You can also jot down other verses in your journal, as you continue to discover verses that are meaningful to your journey.

**My soul is weary with sorrow;
strengthen me according to your word.**

**PSALM 119:28**

**For everything that was written in
the past was written to teach us, so that through
the endurance taught in the Scriptures and the
encouragement they provide we might have hope.**

**ROMANS 15:4**

# Anger

**PROVERBS 15:18**

A hot-tempered person stirs up conflict, but the one who is patient calms a quarrel.

**PROVERBS 19:11**

A person's wisdom yields patience; it is to one's glory to overlook an offense.

**COLOSSIANS 3:13**

Bear with each other and forgive one another if any of you has a grievance against someone. Forgive as the Lord forgave you.

**EPHESIANS 4:26**

"In your anger do not sin": Do not let the sun go down while you are still angry.

**HEBREWS 12:15**

See to it that no one falls short of the grace of God and that no bitter root grows up to cause trouble and defile many.

# Anxiety/fear

**ISAIAH 41:10**

So do not fear, for I am with you; do not be dismayed, for I am your God. I will strengthen you and help you; I will uphold you with my righteous right hand.

**MATTHEW 6:31–33**

So do not worry, saying, "What shall we eat?" or "What shall we drink?" or "What shall we wear?" For the pagans run after all these things, and your heavenly Father knows that you need them. But seek first his kingdom and his righteousness, and all these things will be given to you as well.

**PHILIPPIANS 4:6–7**

Do not be anxious about anything, but in every situation, by prayer and petition, with thanksgiving, present your requests to God. And the peace of God, which transcends all understanding, will guard your hearts and your minds in Christ Jesus.

# God's faithfulness

## NUMBERS 23:19
God is not human, that he should lie, not a human being, that he should change his mind. Does he speak and then not act? Does he promise and not fulfill?

## PSALM 119:89–90
Your word, LORD, is eternal; it stands firm in the heavens. Your faithfulness continues through all generations; you established the earth, and it endures.

## PSALM 91:4
He will cover you with his feathers, and under his wings you will find refuge; his faithfulness will be your shield and rampart.

## 2 THESSALONIANS 3:3
But the Lord is faithful, and he will strengthen you and protect you from the evil one.

## 2 THESSALONIANS 3:3
If we are faithless, he remains faithful, for he cannot disown himself.

# God's love

## PSALM 86:15
But you, Lord, are a compassionate and gracious God, slow to anger, abounding in love and faithfulness.

## ZEPHANIAH 3:17
The LORD your God is with you, the Mighty Warrior who saves. He will take great delight in you; in his love he will no longer rebuke you, but will rejoice over you with singing.

## JOHN 3:16
For God so loved the world that he gave his one and only Son, that whoever believes in him shall not perish but have eternal life.

## ROMANS 8:38–39
For I am convinced that neither death nor life, ... nor anything else in all creation, will be able to separate us from the love of God that is in Christ Jesus our Lord.

# Hope

**PSALM 33:20–22**

We wait in hope for the LORD; he is our help and our shield. In him our hearts rejoice, for we trust in his holy name. May your unfailing love be with us, LORD, even as we put our hope in you.

**PSALM 40:1–2**

I waited patiently for the LORD; he turned to me and heard my cry. He lifted me out of the slimy pit, out of the mud and mire; he set my feet on a rock and gave me a firm place to stand.

**ISAIAH 40:28, 30–31A**

Do you not know? Have you not heard? The LORD is the everlasting God, the Creator of the ends of the earth. He will not grow tired or weary, and his understanding no one can fathom. ... Even youths grow tired and weary, and young men stumble and fall; but those who hope in the LORD will renew their strength.

# Loneliness

**PSALM 23:4**

Even though I walk through the darkest valley, I will fear no evil, for you are with me; your rod and your staff, they comfort me.

**PSALM 25:16**

Turn to me and be gracious to me, for I am lonely and afflicted.

**PSALM 68:5**

A father to the fatherless, a defender of widows, is God in his holy dwelling.

**ISAIAH 43:2**

When you pass through the waters, I will be with you; and when you pass through the rivers, they will not sweep over you. When you walk through the fire, you will not be burned; the flames will not set you ablaze.

**HEBREWS 10:25**

And let us not neglect our meeting together, as some people do, but encourage one another, especially now that the day of his return is drawing near. (NLT)

# Regret/guilt

## PSALM 103:8–12

The LORD is compassionate and gracious, slow to anger, abounding in love. He will not always accuse, nor will he harbor his anger forever; he does not treat us as our sins deserve or repay us according to our iniquities. For as high as the heavens are above the earth, so great is his love for those who fear him; as far as the east is from the west, so far has he removed our transgressions from us.

## PSALM 32:5

I acknowledged my sin to you and did not cover up my iniquity. I said, "I will confess my transgressions to the LORD." And you forgave the guilt of my sin.

## ROMANS 8:1

Therefore, there is now no condemnation for those who are in Christ Jesus.

## 1 JOHN 1:9

If we confess our sins, he is faithful and just and will forgive us our sins and purify us from all unrighteousness.

# Sadness

**PSALM 42:5**

Why, my soul, are you downcast? Why so disturbed within me? Put your hope in God, for I will yet praise him, my Savior and my God.

**PSALM 147:3**

He heals the brokenhearted and binds up their wounds.

**MATTHEW 11:28**

Come to me, all you who are weary and burdened, and I will give you rest.

**PSALM 42:5**

Why, my soul, are you downcast? Why so disturbed within me? Put your hope in God, for I will yet praise him, my Savior and my God.

**PSALM 147:3**

He heals the brokenhearted and binds up their wounds.

**MATTHEW 11:28**

Come to me, all you who are weary and burdened, and I will give you rest.

**JOHN 16:33B**

In this world you will have trouble. But take heart! I have overcome the world.

**REVELATION 7:16–17**

"Never again will they hunger; never again will they thirst. The sun will not beat down on them," nor any scorching heat. For the Lamb at the center of the throne will be their shepherd; "he will lead them to springs of living water." "And God will wipe away every tear from their eyes."

# A word of
## *Encouragement*

Every person's journey is unique. Return to your guided journal often. Reflect on your situation and pray for God to use your journaling to help guide your journey. With each reflection, you can take another step. One step, one page at a time.

# What's next on your journey?

As you continue to grieve, grow, mourn, and heal, consider taking one of these next steps.

# Join a
## GriefShare® group

Whether you've attended a group before or this is your first time, joining a 13-week GriefShare support group is a great way to continue your healing journey.

## Groups meet both in person and online. You can expect:

**Understanding** – People have an idea of how you're feeling because they're facing similar challenges.

**Encouragement** – It's comforting to know you're not alone and to gain strength from the Bible.

**Answers** – You'll learn what to expect in grief and how long it lasts, and get answers to other questions.

**Good advice** – You'll hear from respected counselors and pastors on how to deal with the stresses of grief.

**A structured approach** – GriefShare provides stability with its video teaching, group discussions, and personal workbook.

Find a group today at:
**GRIEFSHARE.ORG**

# Why people love

**People have said that joining a GriefShare group was the best decision they made on their healing journey. Here's why:**

*"It was a safe place I could go to tell my story, cry, and laugh, and I didn't feel judged."* – SUE

*"Being able to hear stories about what people are going through [showed me] I'm not the only one going through this."* – JENILEE

*"I was never taught how to grieve, and GriefShare helped me do that."* – CARL

*"GriefShare has given me the tools to get through what will come."* – KAREN

*"I would not have survived the first year without GriefShare."* – JEANNINE

Join a group today at:
**GRIEFSHARE.ORG**

# Volunteer to help with

## Grief✦Share®

**Your GriefShare group is a great place to give back**

- Serving others can aid your healing process
- Help out with snacks, publicity, or the greeting table
- Talk with your leader about where you'd best fit

**TALK TO YOUR GRIEFSHARE LEADER TODAY**

# Host a

# GriefShare® ministry

**If your church doesn't have a GriefShare group, here's how to get started:**

1. Learn more about GriefShare on our website
2. Contact a GriefShare coach to get started
3. Present the idea to your pastor and talk about your role

Learn how to host a group (online or in person):
**GRIEFSHARE.ORG/HOST-A-GROUP**

# Continue your healing
## *Journey*

**Scan the code to learn more!**